Making Wa\

By Jenny Mosley and Helen Sonnet

Making Waves
MT00821
ISBN-13: 978 1 85503 357 3
© Jenny Mosley and Helen Sonnet
© Illustrations Mark Cripps
Photography © Stills
First published 2002
Reprinted 2002, 2003, 2004, 2005, 2006 (twice), 2007, 2008

Printed in the UK for LDA, Abbeygate House, East Road, Cambridge, CB1 1DB, UK

Acknowledgements

For many years, as a teacher, youth leader, drama therapist and university lecturer, I have used parachute games. They are such fun! I am therefore indebted to all the people who have contributed ideas over the years. It's not possible to thank everyone individually. However, I would like to say a big thank you to Lizzie Yauner and Gerry Wood. They attended my 7-day SENJIT course at London University, and on the follow-up day we invented new games and ideas. The boa constrictor is one of theirs.

Your own groups will also offer you a rich fund of ideas once you get going with your parachute. So, good luck and have lots of fun.

Jenny Mosley

Contents

Introduction

Parachute games provide an opportunity for enjoyable, positive, sharing activities, ideal as part of a team-building programme. They stimulate the senses, offer different environments underneath or on top of the canopy, and teach new skills. Players have to co-operate to produce the desired result and all share in the success they achieve when they bring the parachute to life. The excitement, fun and camaraderie engendered by these activities ensure that parachute sessions are eagerly anticipated by all concerned.

The games and activities in this book include a selection of favourites collected from teachers and youth leaders, and original ideas from the authors. Some games are highly energetic, while others require concentration and still others are calm and relaxing. For ease of reference, the games are divided into different sections by theme. The games can be adapted to suit teachers, youth workers and instructors – in fact any groupwork leaders.

As the children become adept at handling the parachute they will use their imaginations to suggest modifications to the existing games or want to try out activities they have devised themselves.

Getting started

This section introduces the canopy to the children and aims to familiarise them with routine parachute movements and positions. Working together in the way needed for parachute games will probably be a new concept for the children and they will need to practise before they become proficient. Although the children may be impatient to play games, it is a good idea to take time at this stage to teach the basic parachute skills thoroughly. Once the children see what they can accomplish by co-ordinating their movements, they will feel confident, excited and eager to try new manoeuvres.

Starting off

Resources
None

What to do
Let the children help to open out the parachute and lay it on the ground. They can do this by standing around the parachute, facing away from it. They grasp the parachute firmly with both hands behind them and walk forward until the canopy is fully opened out. Ask them to stand evenly spaced around the parachute, then lift it with both hands to waist height.

Spend several minutes letting the children test the feel of the parachute by pulling it taut. Instruct them to hold the parachute in the correct way, practising the thumbs-up grip (thumbs above the parachute, fingers underneath) and the thumbs-down grip (thumbs under the parachute, fingers above). If the parachute you are using does not have a handle for every child in the group, each child could hold the edge of the parachute. This way it is fair for everyone. Get them to practise following instructions together – such as 'All take a step to the left/right'. Ask the children to move in a clockwise/anti-clockwise direction, at first slowly, then gradually speeding up. Practise stopping together without bumping into one another. Also, ask the children to hold the parachute at different levels – near the ground, waist high, at shoulder height and above their heads.

Encourages
Familiarity with the parachute, listening skills, following instructions, working together as a group

Making waves

Resources
None

What to do
Ask the children to shake the parachute randomly to create ripples across the surface. Tell them they are making waves. Get them to practise making gentle and more vigorous movements to represent a calm or stormy sea. Also, practise these movements kneeling and sitting, so they become accustomed to handling the parachute in different positions. Let four children at a time sit underneath the parachute to see the effects of the waves above them.

Encourages
Practising parachute positions, working together as a group

Making a mushroom

Resources
None

What to do
Ask the children to take two steps towards the centre so that the parachute sags. Tell them that on the count of 'One, two, three, up' they are to raise their arms quickly above their heads together, to make the parachute mushroom upwards. Practise this movement, letting the children take turns to count, until they are competent. Once the children have mastered making mushrooms, they can take turns to sit underneath in groups of 3 or 4 while the others make a mushroom.

Encourages
Listening skills, turn-taking, working together

Up, up and away 1

Resources
None

What to do
When the children can make a perfect mushroom, instruct them to let go of the parachute on your command, with a warning that they must respond immediately when you speak. The parachute will rise up into the air, then float down again. Make sure it is not too windy if you do this outside. Practise this several times with the children and finish off by asking them to crouch together in the centre to let the parachute fall over all of them.

Encourages
Listening skills, following instructions, working together, fun

Up, up and away 2

Resources
None

What to do
The children hold the parachute firmly, with the thumbs-up grip. They walk backwards until the parachute is fully extended, then lean back, pulling on the parachute to make it taut. On the count of five, all the children release the parachute, making it jerk upwards.

Encourages
Listening skills, following instructions, working together, co-ordinating movements, fun

Up and down

Resources
None

What to do
The children stand around the parachute, holding it at waist height. On your command, they raise the parachute to head height and hold it there until you tell them to lower it again. You can also tell them to lower it from the starting position until it is at knee level. The children must listen to your commands of 'Raise' or 'Lower' and respond appropriately. To keep them alert, try varying the pace at which you give the commands.

Encourages
Concentration, observation, listening skills, following instructions, working as a group, fun

Pass the parachute along

Resources
None

What to do
The children stand around the parachute and hold it at waist height. They pull the parachute tight and, keeping a steady rhythm, pass it to their right so that it travels in an anti-clockwise direction around the circle. You can tell the children to move it slowly at first, then speed up the pace. Ask the children to stop and change direction, passing the parachute clockwise around the circle.

Encourages
Listening skills, concentration, observation, working together

All turn around

Resources
A stopwatch

What to do
Ask the children to stand with their backs to the parachute, holding it taut with both hands behind them. One child lets go of the parachute with their left hand, turns to face the parachute and holds it again in both hands. When this movement is completed, the child to the left turns to face the parachute and so on around the circle in a clockwise direction. The children must not move until the previous child has completed their move. Time the children to see how quickly they can do this around the circle. Repeat in the opposite direction.

Encourages
Concentration, observation, turn-taking, working as a group

Move along round

Resources
None

What to do
The children hold the parachute at waist height and make waves on the surface. A child is chosen to begin the activity. They move around the outside of the others. This child chooses another child and taps them on the shoulder, taking their position at the parachute. The second child continues around the parachute and selects a third child to take their place, and so on. You can make this more interesting by asking the children to instruct their chosen player in the manner in which they must move – for example hop, jump, crawl, skip.

Encourages
Concentration, observation, turn-taking

Right hand, left hand

Resources
None

What to do
The children hold the parachute in their right hands, standing sideways on to it. Ask them to walk slowly round in a clockwise direction. Once they have achieved a smooth progress, ask them to walk faster. Tell them to stop, change hands and direction, and repeat the process. Continue the activity, changing direction and mode of movement by introducing skipping, hopping, jumping and so on.

Encourages
Co-ordinating movement, following instruction, concentration, observation

17

Greetings

Resources
None

What to do
Instruct the children that when the parachute mushrooms, they will take it in turns around the circle to shout a greeting to someone else. Discuss before playing what sort of things they might say; for example, 'Hello ..., have a nice day.' When the parachute descends below head height, they should stop and wait for the next mushroom before starting again.

Encourages
Turn-taking, imagination, positive self-focus

Simon says

Resources
None

What to do
The children hold the parachute at waist height to begin the game. The activity proceeds in the usual way, with the children responding only to commands that are preceded by 'Simon says'. They are out if they make a mistake. Obviously, you will have to consider movements that are possible with the parachute. These might include raising or lowering the parachute, moving available body parts, saying something and so on. Each time a child is out, the remaining children space themselves out around the parachute. The game continues until you feel that you have reached the minimum number of children left to support the parachute and carry out the activities.

Encourages
Listening skills, concentration, fun

Moving on

By the time the children have completed all the previous activities, they should be ready to play parachute games. It is worth ensuring that the children are competent at the various manoeuvres; otherwise they will be preoccupied with trying to carry out the movements, which will make game-playing a frustrating experience for all concerned.

Swapping places

Now the children are ready to begin playing games, start with simple place swapping. Once the children have experienced this activity, you can add more demanding details. The games in this section are particularly good for encouraging turn-taking and ensuring that each child has an equal opportunity to participate and enjoy positive attention. The variations of place swapping include a focus on drama skills and motor skills.

Place swap

Resources
None

What to do
Call out the names of two children on opposite sides of the parachute. When the children have made the parachute mushroom, the named children swap places by running under the parachute. Continue until all the children have had a turn.

Encourages
Turn-taking, listening skills, observation, fun

Alphabetical order

Resources
None

What to do
This is a more complex version of **Place swap** in which the children have to change places in alphabetical order. This should be done using the initial letter of first names, but if you have several children with the same name, use surnames instead. The class have to work out amongst themselves who are the next children to swap places.

Encourages
Concentration, thinking skills, observation

Move in this way

Resources
None

What to do
In this version of **Place swap**, you tell the children changing places how to move under the parachute mushroom. This could be, for example, hopping on one foot, jumping, on tip-toes, walking backwards (carefully), on hands and knees, bunny jumping or walking sideways. Ask the children for their ideas about different ways to move.

Encourages
Listening skills, physical skills, fun

A nod and a wink

Resources
None

What to do
In this version of **Place swap**, the children choose whom they will change with. They signal to the child they wish to swap places with in a non-verbal manner – for example with a wink or a nod. They take turns to do this around the circle.

Encourages
Observation, concentration, imagination, fun

Boys and girls

Resources
None

What to do
The children swap places by gender in this version. All the girls or all the boys leave their places and cross under the parachute to new positions. If you think this would involve too many children at once, you can also select categories –for example all the boys with brown eyes, or all the girls with their hair up.

Encourages
Concentration, listening skills, fun

Stop and greet

Resources

None

What to do

The children swapping places stop in the centre of the circle, under the mushroom, to greet each other. They can do this in turn around the circle, the child whose turn it is choosing whom to swap places with and what the greeting should be. Examples are shaking hands, a high five, kissing cheeks in the French greeting, Indian salaam, and bowing as the Japanese do. Ask the children if they can think of any others.

Encourages

Turn-taking, imagination, positive focus, fun

Pretend to be

Resources
Prepared list

What to do
Have a prepared list of people and animals with distinctive ways of moving. Give each pair of children a different mime to carry out when swapping places. They could mime being ballet dancers, tennis players, old people, toddlers learning to walk, monkeys, kangaroos, dogs, frogs and so on.

Encourages
Imagination, positive focus, turn-taking, fun

Swapping sets

Resources
List of categories

What to do
This variation of **Place swap** uses different categories to select the players. When the parachute mushrooms, call a category – for example anyone with a birthday in May. All the children who fit into that category change places. Other categories could be anyone who has a dog as a pet or anyone with brown eyes. You will need to do a little research regarding categories as you do not want all the children to let go of the parachute at the same time. Include some fun categories such as anyone who loves Brussels sprouts or anyone who hates pop music.

Encourages
Listening skills, observation, concentration, fun

Your number is up

Resources
None

What to do
Number the children 1 to 6 around the circle. When the parachute mushrooms, call out one or more numbers. All the children whose number has been called swap places.

Encourages
Listening skills, concentration, observation, turn-taking

Around and back

Resources
None

What to do
In this version of **Place swap**, the children named have to run around the outside of the circle when the parachute mushrooms. When they reach their places again, they can cross under the mushroom.

Encourages
Physical activity, turn-taking

Taking steps

Resources
List of activities, rope, ball

What to do
Prepare a list of activities that children have to carry out as they swap places. These could include skipping (with a rope) under the mushroom, then handing the rope to another child who has to skip back to the vacant place. The children could bounce a ball as they cross, handing it over to the next child; or hold the ball between their knees and jump across, trying not to drop the ball. Ask the children for suggestions of different activities they could use.

Encourages
Physical skills, turn-taking, positive focus

Tent games

The games in this section are a mixture of active and quieter games. The latter are very useful for encouraging group cohesion and creating a positive atmosphere and are therefore ideal for enhancing group dynamics. These particular games focus on turn-taking and thinking skills.

Making a tent

Resources
None

What to do
Tell the children to crouch around the edge of the parachute. On the count of 'One, two, three, up', the children make the parachute mushroom, take a step inwards, pull the parachute behind them and sit on the edge. One child stands in the centre as the tent pole, holding up the parachute.

Encourages
Listening skills, following instructions, co-ordinating movement, working together

Check the tent pole

Resources
None

What to do
Begin this game by making a tent. The 'tent pole' names another child. On the count of 'One, two, three, go', they swap places before the tent collapses.

Encourages
Concentration, positive focus, fun

Rounds

Resources
None

What to do
While the children are sitting in the tent they can complete rounds – for example 'My favourite food is ... '.

Encourages
Turn-taking, positive focus, talking in a group

Story-telling

Resources
None

What to do
The children can tell a story around the circle while they sit in the tent. Each child adds a sentence to the story.

Encourages
Turn-taking, language skills, imagination, talking in a group, fun

Sing a song

Resources
None

What to do
Ask the children to sing a song together while they sit in the tent. Make sure you choose one they all know. See if anyone can suggest another familiar song that you could teach them all.

Encourages
Team-building, enjoyment

Find my favourite

Resources
None

What to do
Once inside the tent, the children take turns to think of something – for example 'my favourite food', an animal, or a pop group. The other children ask questions about the subject and try to guess the correct answer.

Encourages
Imagination, turn-taking, positive focus, talking in a group

Lively lists

Resources
None

What to do
While the children are sitting in the tent, they can play a memory game such as 'I went camping and took ...' around the circle. Each child must remember all the items previously said and add a new item to the list. When a child is unable to complete the list, they begin again.

Encourages
Turn-taking, memory skills, talking in a group

Guess who's in the tent

Resources
None

What to do
Choose one child to be the guesser. They turn their back on the other children, who move around the parachute to change their positions, then make a tent. Once the children are hidden inside the tent, the child who is guessing walks around the parachute, tapping each occupant in turn on the shoulder. When a child is tapped they say, 'I like sitting inside the tent.' The child outside has to listen to the voice and try to guess the identity of the speaker. They can ask the speaker to repeat the statement once more. The object of the game is to guess as many correct identities as possible. If a child guesses incorrectly or fails to make a guess, they are out. The children come out of the tent, a new guesser is chosen and the game begins again.

Encourages
Positive focus, listening skills, concentration, fun

In and out of the tent

Resources
None

What to do
Ask the children to stand around the parachute, holding it at waist height with their hands crossed (right over left). On the count of 'One, two, three, go', everyone raises their arms and turns through 180 degrees to their right, letting go of the parachute with their right hand and thereby uncrossing their arms. Taking hold of the parachute with both hands, they take a step towards the centre, pulling the parachute over them to make a tent. They should all be facing outwards at this point. The procedure is then reversed so that all the players return to their original positions. This is quite a complicated manoeuvre, so save it until the children are proficient at handling the parachute.

Encourages
Following instructions, co-ordinating movement, fun

Active games

The games in this section focus on physical activity, including high-energy interactive games. They can be used either to burn off surplus energy when the children seem restless or to energise the children if they are lethargic. The games are fun, exciting and inviting, encouraging all to participate.

Flatten the hill

Resources
None

What to do
Choose two children standing on opposite sides of the parachute to 'flatten the hill'. Tell the rest to make the parachute mushroom, then quickly pull the edges down and kneel on them. This action will trap air in the parachute to form a hill. The two children then climb onto the parachute and jump on it to squeeze out the air. Continue until all the children have had a turn.

Encourages
Turn-taking, positive focus, fun

Tunnelling

Resources
None

What to do
The children take turns to tunnel under the parachute when it is on the ground and held in place by the others. It is best to begin this game with a taut parachute as that makes it easier for the children to swap places. Let all the children have a turn, then repeat the process. This time, ask the children holding the parachute to create waves and ripples to disorientate the tunnellers.

Encourages
Concentration, fun

The tortoise

Resources
None

What to do
The parachute is the shell of a tortoise. Choose half of the group to get underneath on their hands and knees, all facing the same way. They must try to move together to create the tortoise. The rest of the group watch and give encouragement. They then reverse roles.

Encourages
Co-ordinating movement, working together, fun

Search for treasure

Resources
Tennis ball

What to do
The parachute is laid on the ground. The children make waves and a small ball is rolled underneath. A child is chosen to tunnel under the parachute and try to retrieve the ball. Go round the circle until every child has had a turn.

Encourages
Concentration, turn-taking, fun

Treasure chest

Resources
A box of small items that can be identified by touch – for example pencil, bulldog clip, spoon, brush

What to do
With the children's help, fill a box with small items, noting down all the things you have put in. There need to be enough items for each child to have one. Place the box in the centre, under the parachute. Choose two children and tell them which items they have to retrieve from the box when the parachute mushrooms. They must be back in their places before the mushroom comes down. Play the game until all the children have had a turn.

Encourages
Turn-taking, physical activity, fun

Whose shoes?

Resources
None

What to do
Before you begin this game, ask all the children to stand in a circle and look at each other's shoes. Choose a child to sit under the centre of the parachute, which is draped over the child. The other children quickly move left or right around the parachute to change their positions. The children grasp the parachute in both hands and raise it to knee level, making sure that the child underneath can see only their legs and feet. Tap one child on the shoulder. They begin to march on the spot. The child in the centre has to guess the marcher's identity from their shoes. If they are successful, the children swap places. If not, the child guessing has one more turn.

Encourages
Observation, memory skills, fun

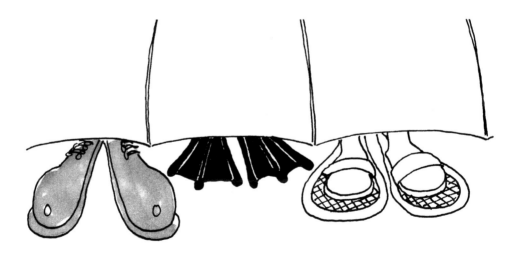

Fly the kite

Resources
None

What to do
You need plenty of space for this activity, so it is best played outside. The parachute is laid on the ground at one end of the playing area. All the children hold one side of the parachute with one hand. On the command of 'Go', the children begin to run down the length of the playing area, holding the parachute up high behind them so that it resembles a kite in the wind.

Encourages
Physical activity, working together, fun

Out in a boat

Resources
None

What to do
The parachute is laid on the ground to form a pond, with all the children seated around it. Two or three children are chosen for the boat ride, and sit or lie in the centre. The rest of the children create ripples and waves on the pond that grow in intensity and then gradually subside to represent a storm. Continue with the game until all the children have had a turn in the boat.

Encourages
Turn-taking, working together, fun

Presents

Resources
A small cardboard box, preferably gift wrapped

What to do
The children hold the parachute at waist height. The box is placed on the parachute and a child is chosen to receive the present. The other children then tilt and ripple the parachute to move the box to the named child. When this has been achieved, the child decides what present they would like the box to contain, then names another child to receive a present. The game continues until all the children have had a turn.

Encourages
Positive focus, concentration, co-ordinating movement, working together

Around the inside

Resources
None

What to do
The children stand holding the parachute at waist height. On the count of three they make a mushroom. A chosen child runs around the inside of the circle and back to their place before the mushroom collapses. With smaller circles or older children you can make the game more exciting by seeing how many children can complete the run in one mushroom.

Encourages
Physical activity, positive focus, fun

Chain letter

Resources
A large packet with a plain cover and a pen/pencil

What to do
Attach the pen to the packet with a length of ribbon. The children stand, holding the parachute at waist height. You write the name of a child on the packet and put it on the parachute. The children tilt and ripple the parachute to deliver the 'letter' to the named child. That child then writes a new name underneath their own and the letter is delivered to the next child. The game continues until all the children's names have been written on the letter.

Encourages
Turn-taking, concentration, observation, co-ordinating movement, working together

Sock snatch •

Resources
None

What to do
The children remove their shoes and kneel on the parachute. On your command, the children try to grab the socks of other children without losing their own. Once a child has lost both socks, they must get off the parachute. The winner is the child who has collected the most socks. Allow a set time for this game. This game is best played with small groups.

Encourages
Physical activity, concentration, fun

Sharks

Resources
None

What to do
The children sit around the parachute with their legs underneath. They pretend the parachute is the sea and shake the edge to make waves. A child is chosen to be the shark and goes underneath the parachute. The shark pushes their hands up under the parachute to look like a fin, whilst moving around. The shark selects a victim by pulling someone's feet. The victim lets out a yell and disappears beneath the waves to replace the shark, who then becomes a bather.

Encourages
Observation, positive focus, fun

Cat and mouse

Resources
None

What to do
The children stand around the parachute, holding it at waist height. A child is chosen to be the mouse and goes underneath the parachute. A cat is also chosen; they go on top of the parachute. The cat tries to catch the mouse, but the other children make the parachute billow and ripple to disguise the mouse's whereabouts. If the cat has difficulty in locating the mouse, after a while the children can briefly lower the parachute to show the outline of the child underneath. You can also play this game with several cats and mice.

Encourages
Physical activity, co-ordinating movement, team-building, observation, fun

Language and song

The games in this section focus on the children's imagination and on encouraging their listening and language skills. Some games provide group chants or the opportunity to sing together, which is an enjoyable and uplifting experience, especially on a dull, dreary day.

Heads and shoulders

Resources
None

What to do
Using the thumbs-down grip, the children move the level of the parachute to correspond to the following song:

> Heads and shoulders, knees and toes, knees and toes.
> Heads and shoulders, knees and toes, knees and toes.
> And eyes and ears and mouth and nose.
> Heads and shoulders, knees and toes, knees and toes.

Encourages
Observation, concentration, group-singing, fun

Underground whispers

Resources
None

What to do
The children lie under the parachute with their heads to the centre and feet in the air. They pull the parachute over their feet to make a tent. When they have done this, they can play a game of Chinese whispers. One child begins by whispering a sentence to the child on their left. The whisper is sent from child to child until it gets back to the first child, who compares it to the original sentence to see if and how it has changed.

Encourages
Listening skills, co-operation, fun

The boa constrictor

Resources
None

What to do
To the tune of 'Here we go round the mulberry bush', the children sing:

> The boa constrictor eats me up, eats me up, eats me up.
> The boa constrictor eats me up – all the way to my ankles.

The parachute is held at ankle level. They repeat the song, substituting 'knees' for 'ankles', then 'waist' and 'neck'. As the song progresses to knees, waist and neck, the parachute is gradually raised. The final verse ends 'The boa constrictor swallows me whole', and the children pull the parachute right over themselves.

Encourages
Co-ordinating movement, concentration, observation

Clues

Resources
A box of small familiar items. Prior to the lesson, make sure that you work out the clues that you will use.

What to do
Fill a box with familiar items without letting the children see them. Place the box in the centre under the parachute. Choose two children to retrieve an item from the box when the parachute mushrooms. Give the children a clue to the object's identity without naming it – for example something to remove tangles from your hair (hairbrush), something to use to make yourself clean (flannel), something you need to prepare baked beans (saucepan), something you need to take your pet out (dog lead). Continue with the game until all the children have had a turn.

Encourages
Listening skills, observation, concentration, fun

Row the boat 1

Resources
None

What to do
The children sit cross-legged around the edge of the parachute. They grasp the parachute in both hands and gently pull it back and forth to represent rowing a boat. They try to set up a rhythmic movement and sing:

> Row, row, row the boat, gently down the stream.
> Merrily, merrily, merrily, merrily, life is but a dream.

Encourages
Co-ordinating movement, working together, observation, concentration

Row the boat 2

Resources
None

What to do
While the children are rowing, choose one child to walk around the outside of the circle, moving their arms in a rowing motion. The children can take turns at this. Also, speed up or slow down the rhythm of the song.

Encourages
Co-ordinating movement, working together, positive focus, observation, concentration

The weather today

Resources
Flipchart and pen

What to do
Ask the children to brainstorm all the weather conditions they can think of and write them down on the flipchart. The children are told to imagine the parachute is a pond. They stand around the parachute and hold it at waist height. They choose a child and chant the following rhyme to them:

> [Child's name (x 2)], tell us all
> Is it calm or is there a squall?
> Is it sunny or is it grey?
> What's the weather like today?

The child named chooses one of the weather conditions and the children decide how this will affect the pond. They then create the desired effect on the parachute. The game continues with a different child choosing.

Encourages
Positive focus, imagination, observation, turn-taking

Pond story

Resources
None

What to do
The children sit around the parachute with their legs underneath. Ask them to imagine that the parachute is a pond and explain that they are to represent activity in and on the pond as you talk them through a story.

It is a lovely, warm summer's day. A gentle breeze ripples the surface of the pond. (*The children make ripples on the surface of the parachute.*) Fish swim about, in and out of the pondweed. (*The children wiggle their feet to represent fish.*) Frogs jump in the water. (*The children make jumping movements with their feet.*) Birds dive into the water to catch fish. (*Choose two or three children to represent the birds. They tunnel under the parachute and out the other side.*) On the banks, the anglers sit, casting their lines into the water. (*Choose two children to mime the people fishing.*) A dog jumps into the water to fetch a stick. (*Choose two children to mime the dog and its owner.*) Clouds are starting to form in the sky and the wind is getting stronger and stronger. Now there is a raging storm. The waves on the pond are growing bigger and more violent. (*The children make bigger and stronger waves with the parachute.*) Slowly the storm passes over and the waves die down until it is calm and the pond is as still as a sheet of glass. (*The children gradually make the waves more gentle and end by pulling the parachute taut and still.*)

Encourages
Listening skills, concentration, observation, imagination

Frog in the middle

Resources
None

What to do
The parachute is spread out on the floor to represent a lily pad. The children kneel around the edge. One child is chosen to be the frog and sit in the middle. The children all chant:

> Froggy, froggy, we're lonely and sad,
> Can we come and share your pad?

The frog responds with 'Only if you ...', naming a category. These could include, for example, have an 'r' in your name, have a pet cat, have a birthday in March, have an older brother, live in a particular road, have a red car. All the children who fit into the category are allowed to move one knee forward. The game continues until one child reaches and touches the crouching frog. That child becomes the frog and the game begins again.

Encourages
Imagination, observation, concentration, fun

Butterflies

Resources

None

What to do

Two children crouch down together in the centre. The other children cover them with the parachute so that they are completely hidden from view. As they do this they chant:

> Caterpillar, caterpillar, it's the month of June,
> You're warm and cosy in your cocoon.
> Butterfly, butterfly, now it's July,
> And time for you to come out and fly.

The children in the parachute unwrap themselves and 'fly' off. Repeat with another pair until everyone has had a turn.

Encourages

Turn-taking, positive focus, fun

Old MacDonald

Resources
None

What to do
The children sing the song 'Old MacDonald had a farm'. Before each verse, choose three or four children to go under the parachute and mime being the animal named. On the second line of the song, the children lift up the parachute to allow the animals to go underneath. They mime the actions and make the noises of the animal, returning to their places on the last line of the verse.

Encourages
Turn-taking, positive focus, imagination, fun

Dragon in the cave

Resources
None

What to do
A child is chosen to be the dragon in the cave and sits down under the parachute. The other children crouch down and hold the edge of the parachute. They call to the dragon:

> Fiery dragon in your cold, dark cave,
> Whom will you choose to be bold and brave?

The dragon names two children. On the count of three, the children stand and make the parachute mushroom. The two children named try to cross the cave safely while the dragon tries to catch one of them. If the dragon is successful, the child who has been caught becomes the new dragon. If neither child is caught, the process is repeated and two different children are chosen. If the dragon fails to capture a victim after three attempts, a new dragon is chosen.

Encourages
Physical activity, positive focus, fun

Ball games

The games in this section have a particular focus on parachute movement skills and require considerable concentration. The children must co-operate and work together to achieve a goal. These are ideal team-building activities. The games are active, exciting and very inviting to all children, encouraging them to participate and be part of the fun.

Excitaball

Resources
A large, light ball

What to do
The children stand around the parachute, holding it at waist height. Place the ball in the middle and let the children play with the parachute, creating ripples and waves or tilting it to see how the ball moves.

Encourages
Co-ordinating movement, working together

Side to side

Resources
A large, light ball

What to do
The children stand around the parachute, holding it firmly at waist height. They pull it taut. Practise a jerking movement until they can do this in unison. This involves a rapid movement to the right, then left, or vice versa. You will need to count them in and call 'right – left' to help them perfect this action. Once the children have mastered the movement, place the ball on the parachute and let them jerk it around.

Encourages
Listening skills, co-ordinating movement, working together, fun

Jumping bean

Resources
A large, light ball

What to do
The children hold the parachute firmly at waist height in the thumbs-up grip. They use a flicking motion up and down with their wrists and pull back slightly to snap the parachute and make it jump. It is probably best to count them in, then call 'up – down' to help them achieve unison of movement. When you feel that they are ready, place the ball on the parachute.

Encourages
Listening skills, working together, co-ordinating movement, concentration

Under the mushroom

Resources
A large, light ball

What to do
The children create a mushroom with the parachute. One child holds the ball and calls to another child on the opposite side of the circle. The first child then throws the ball to the child they have called. The process is continued, a third child being named, and so on, and the ball is sent backwards and forwards under the mushroom between the children. When the parachute descends, the children will have to suspend play until they have created another mushroom.

Encourages
Turn-taking, motor skills, fun

Snap and catch

Resources
A sponge ball

What to do
The children kneel around the parachute. Choose three children to kneel in the centre of the parachute, facing the outside. Place the sponge ball near the edge of the parachute and ask the children near it to make it jump into the air using the wrist-snap movement (see page 63). The children in the centre have to try to catch the ball. If one is successful, they change places with a child on the outside of the parachute. If none of the children catches the ball, it is made to jump again by the children nearest to it. Change the children in the centre after three unsuccessful attempts at catching.

Encourages
Observation, concentration, gross motor skills, fun

Round the circle

Resources
A large, light ball

What to do
The children stand around the parachute, holding it at waist height. They have to try to get the ball to travel round near the edge of the parachute by varying its height. The parachute needs to be held taut for this game. It takes quite a bit of practice, but with concentration the children raise or lower their arms to create a wave effect and send the ball rolling smoothly round. Once they have perfected their technique, they can see how quickly they can get the ball rolling.

Encourages
Observation, concentration, co-ordinating movement, working together

High ball

Resources
A large, light ball

What to do
The children stand around the parachute, holding it at waist height. The ball is placed in the middle and the children pull the parachute outwards and upwards to send the ball as high as possible. It is a good idea to count them in so that they all pull at the same time.

Encourages
Concentration, observation, co-ordinating movement, working together

Shaking all over

Resources
Twenty small, soft balls

What to do
The children stand around the parachute, holding it at waist height. Place the soft balls on the parachute. Ask the children to see how quickly they can shake all the balls off.

Encourages
Concentration, co-ordinating movement, working together, fun

Bucket ball

Resources
Ten tennis balls and a bucket

What to do
The children sit around the parachute, holding it taut. Place the bucket next to one child. Place a tennis ball on the parachute and ask the children to manoeuvre it into the bucket. Continue until all the balls are in the bucket.

Encourages
Concentration, co-ordinating movement, working together

Shake a score

Resources
A large, light ball

What to do
The children are divided into two teams, A and B. The parachute is divided into two halves by drawing or attaching a line across the diameter. One half is Team A's territory; the other half is Team B's. The children stand, holding the parachute at waist height. The ball is placed in the middle. Team A has to try to shake the ball off over Team B's side and vice versa. Each time a team succeeds, they score a goal and the ball is returned to the centre.

Encourages
Concentration, working together, excitement

On and off

Resources
Ten soft balls

What to do
Divide the children into two teams, A and B. The teams face each other across the parachute, which they hold at waist height. Place the ten soft balls on the parachute and tell Team A they must try to shake the balls off on Team B's side. Team B must try to keep the balls on the parachute. You can either time how long it takes to achieve this or set a time after which you count how many balls are left on the parachute. The teams then reverse roles.

Encourages
Concentration, co-ordinating movement, working together, excitement

Spring cleaning

Resources
Ten soft balls

What to do
The children stand around the parachute, holding it at waist height. Choose two children to go under the parachute. Place the ten soft balls on the parachute. The children underneath have to try to push the balls off while the other children try to keep them on. Allow a set time, then change the children underneath and start again.

Encourages
Concentration, co-ordinating movement, working together, fun

Cross ball

Resources
A large, light ball

What to do
The children stand around the parachute, holding it at waist height. Choose a child (Child A) to begin. Child A places the ball on the parachute. They shout 'To ... ', naming someone on the opposite side of the parachute (this is Child B). The children manoeuvre the parachute to send the ball to Child B, who then shouts 'To ... ', naming the child on the left of Child A. This child, Child C, names the child on the left of Child B and sends the ball to them (they are Child D). The children send the ball backwards and forwards, always to the child on the left of the previous player. Each time they name the child so that everyone knows where the ball has to go.

Encourages
Turn-taking, concentration, co-ordinating movement, working together

Beat the count

Resources
A tennis ball

What to do
You will need to decide prior to playing the game on a countdown that you think will give just sufficient time for the activity. The children stand around the parachute and hold it at waist height. Choose two children. Give a ball to Child A. After the call 'Ready, steady, go', the children lift the parachute up and begin the countdown (e.g. 8, 7, 6 and so on). After 1, they lower the parachute again. As soon as the parachute has been raised, Child A runs underneath and places the ball in the centre, returning afterwards to their place. Only when Child A is back in place can Child B leave their place and retrieve the ball. The object of the game is for both children to be back in place before the parachute is lowered. If the activity is too easy or too hard to achieve, adjust the countdown accordingly.

Encourages
Concentration, turn-taking, fun

Calming and ending games

The games in this section can be used either to calm children down after an exciting and vigorous parachute session or for relaxation. Putting the parachute away can become an ending ritual to bring closure to the activities.

Creative visualisation 1 – feathers

Resources
None

What to do
Ask the children to lie on the floor with their feet towards the centre and covered by the parachute. Tell them to close their eyes. Continue as follows:

> Imagine you are a feather floating in the air. You are very light and fluffy and you are wafting along on a warm and gentle breeze. You glide over the tree tops and hear the leaves rustling on the branches. Far below you can see the neat rectangles of yellow, brown and green fields and the thin silvery line of a river winding its way through the meadows. You feel peaceful and relaxed.

Encourages
Imagination, relaxation

Creative visualisation 2 – leaves

Resources
None

What to do

Ask the children to lie on the floor with their feet towards the centre and covered by the parachute. Tell them to close their eyes. Continue as follows:

> Imagine you are a leaf on the surface of a river. The current is carrying you along, sometimes slowly and sluggishly and sometimes swiftly and strongly. You can hear the music of the river as it flows along and the gentle lapping of the water against the banks. You can see the green, mossy banks and the tall slender reeds and, under the water, the smooth, rounded, multi-coloured pebbles. Silver fish dart or glide between the water weeds and sometimes gently nibble the fronds. You feel calm and relaxed as you glide along.

Encourages
Imagination, relaxation

Creative visualisation 3 – snowflakes

Resources
None

What to do
Ask the children to lie on the floor with their feet towards the centre and covered by the parachute. Tell them to close their eyes. Continue as follows:

> Imagine you are a snowflake drifting slowly down through the air. Everything around you is covered in deep, white snow. You can see the outlines of trees and houses with smoke lazily rising in curling wisps from the chimneys. Sometimes a gust of wind catches you and tosses you back up again. As you get nearer to the ground you can see in the snow tracks of animals and footprints of people. Follow a set of prints in your mind's eye and see where it leads. You reach the ground and settle into the soft, thick carpet of snow. You feel relaxed and still.

Encourages
Imagination, relaxation

Cooling off

Resources
None

What to do
Two children lie on the ground under the parachute while the rest make rapid mushrooms to create a draught underneath. After a set time, they are replaced by two others. Continue until all the children have had a turn.

Encourages
Turn-taking, positive focus, relaxation

Parachute hoist

Resources
None

What to do
Let three or four children lie on the parachute with their feet pointing to the centre. The other children gently lift them a few centimetres from the ground and sway them back and forth.

Encourages
Positive focus, turn-taking, trust, co-operation

Hammocks

Resources
None

What to do
Let the children help to fold up the parachute at the end of a session. When it has been folded into a rectangle, let one child at a time lie on the parachute while several others pick it up and gently swing it from side to side. You could do this with several children after each session, making sure everyone has a turn over a few sessions.

Encourages
Positive focus, turn-taking, trust, co-operation

Roll the parachute

Resources
None

What to do
Lay the parachute on the ground. Ask half the group to kneel on one side of the parachute and the other half to kneel opposite them on the other side of the parachute. Ask the children to hold the material in both hands. Let them roll up the parachute towards the centre, singing to the tune of 'Here we go round the mulberry bush':

This is the way we roll the chute, roll the chute, roll the chute.
This is the way we roll the chute at the end of our parachute playtime.

Encourages
Working together, co-ordinating movement

Training and resources

Jenny Mosley INSET courses

The following courses and workshops are available from a team of highly qualified and experienced consultants, who can be contacted through:

Jenny Mosley Consultancies
28a Gloucester Road
Trowbridge
Wiltshire
BA14 0AA

Tel: 01225 767157
Fax: 01225 755631

Email: circletime@jennymosley.demon.co.uk
Web site: www.circle-time.co.uk

- Promoting happier lunchtimes
- Turn your school round – an introduction
- A whole-school approach to building self-esteem through Circle Time
- Assessing the effectiveness of your self-esteem, anti-bullying and positive behaviour policies
- Raising staff morale through team-building
- Practical activities to maintain and develop the power of Circle Time
- A workshop of games to enrich class and lunchtimes.

Training support for your workplace

The Jenny Mosley Consultancies' well-trained personnel, experienced in all aspects of the Quality Circle Time model, are available to visit your workplace to give courses and workshops to all your teaching and support staff.

We run both closure and in-school days. In the closure day, all staff, teachers, teaching assistants, lunchtime supervisors and administrative staff are invited to explore how to develop team-building and moral values through Golden Rules, incentives and sanctions, and ideas for happier lunchtimes.

During the in-school day the school does not close and the Quality Circle Time method is demonstrated with whole classes of children, observed by a range of staff. In addition to this, Circle Time meetings are held for lunchtime supervisors and an action plan for the school is considered with key members of staff.

Training the trainer courses

Key people may be trained either to go back to their school or their LEA as accredited trainers, responsible for supporting all adults and children in their community through the Jenny Mosley model. For details of ongoing courses contact Jenny Mosley Consultancies on 01225 767157.

Quality Circle Time training manuals and resources

Mosley, J. (1998) *More Quality Circle Time*, LDA
Mosley, J. (1998) *Quality Circle Time*, LDA
Mosley, J. (1993) *Turn Your School Round*, LDA
Mosley, J. and Sonnet, H. (2002) *101 Games For Self-Esteem*, LDA
Mosley, J. and Thorp, G. (2002) *All Year Round*, LDA
Mosley, J. and Thorp, G. (2002) *Playground Games*, LDA
Mosley, J. and Thorp, G. (2002) *Playground Notelets*, LDA
Goldthorpe, M. (1998) *Effective IEPs through Circle Time*, LDA
Goldthorpe, M. (1998) *Poems for Circle Time and Literacy Hour*, LDA
Goldthorpe, M. and Nutt, L. (2000) *Assemblies to Teach Golden Rules*, LDA

Mosley, J. (2000) *Quality Action in Action*, LDA
Mosley, J. (2000) *Quality Circle Time Kit*, LDA
Mosley, J. (1996) *Class Reward Sheets*, LDA
Mosley, J. (1996) *Golden Rules Posters*, LDA
Mosley, J. (1996) *Responsibility Badges*, LDA
Mosley, J. (1996) *Reward Certificates*, LDA
Mosley, J. (1996) *Stickers*, LDA

For information about the full range of Jenny Mosley's books and resources, please ring LDA Customer Services on 01945 463441.